TECHNOLOGY BYTES!

by

RANDY GLASBERGEN

CCC PUBLICATIONS

Published by

CCC Publications
9725 Lurline Avenue
Chatsworth, CA. 91311

Manufactured in the United States of America

Cover © 1996 CCC Publications

Interior Illustrations © 1996 CCC Publications

Cover & Interior art by Randy Glasbergen

Cover/Interior production by Oasis Graphics

ISBN:0-57644-014-1

If your local U.S. bookstore is out of stock, copies of this book may be obtained by mailing check or money order for $5.95 per book (plus $2.75 to cover postage and handling) to: CCC Publications, 9725 Lurline Avenue, Chatsworth, CA. 91311

Pre-publication Edition - 6/96   Second Printing - 9/96   Fourth Printing - 12/99

First Printing - 8/96   Third Printing - 11/96

Top Ten Reasons Why You Should Buy This Book Instead of a New Computer:

10) This book is not educational and no one will expect you to act smarter after buying it.

9) All pages are already typed for you—no keyboard skills necessary!

8) Accessing these pages is up to 10,000% faster than accessing web pages during peak hours.

7) This book is more portable than the lightest laptop and you can read it in the bathtub without frying any vital organs!

6) This book requires no future upgrades or add ons and will not become obsolete as soon as you get it home.

5) Pages of this book will not disappear during a power failure.

4) In 5 years a new computer will only be useful as a paperweight. In 5 years this book will still be a book!

3) Technical support for this book can be summed up in three words: *Wear glasses, stupid!*

2) You can loan this book to your dad without having to explain how to use it.

And the #1 reason why you should buy this book instead of a new computer: **Bill Gates doesn't make a penny from the sale of this book!**

Mrs. Brandobundt whines in a high, squeaky tone and is often mistaken for an incoming fax transmission.

"We installed little monitors because they make all of our problems seem smaller."

Larry tiled his entire bathroom using free disks he received in the mail from CompuServe and America Online.

"Looks like we're the victims of corporate sabotage. Someone has been making decaf!"

"This is Dave. I'm away from my desk right now. Please leave a message and I'll forget to return your call as soon as possible."

"I finally made my stupid computer go faster. I dropped it out the window and it went **REALLY** fast!"

"I never got to see my children grow up. I was on hold."

"Does anybody use the computers at your high school?
I accidentally e-mailed them your diary."

"I introduced the world's first nose-top computer 18 months ago. Sales are slower than originally anticipated."

GLASBERGEN

"If you'd like to press 1, press 3.
If you'd like to press 3, press 8.
If you'd like to press 8, press 5..."

"His full name is ThomasJr@metronet.com but we'll probably call him Tommy."

"Babes love a guy with a big antenna!"

"First he bought his computer a fancy new hard drive and an expensive CD-ROM. Then he bought his computer $2000 worth of new software. Then he bought his computer a diamond necklace..."

"I don't know what to call myself. All the really sexy screen names are already taken!"

"In theory, I like the idea of a paperless office, but did you ever try to blow your nose on a disk?"

"If you want to place an order, press 1. If you want to inquire about a previous order, press 2. If you want your money back press 316790472650192738."

"The World Wide Web is very educational. I learned how to make peach preserves and my husband learned that his parents like to pose for naked pictures."

"Dad, are you calling me from the built-in phone in your new computer? Dad, I can barely hear you! Dad, are you talking into the mouse again?"

"This machine is a printer, a fax, a copier and a scanner. It also automatically collates and distributes office gossip."

"We both have cellular phones, fax machines, e-mail, voice mail and pagers—so why can't we communicate with each other???"

"I found the problem. This unit was manufactured on February 20th, so it's a Pisces. You can network a Pisces with a Scorpio or Aquarius, but **NEVER** with a Taurus or Capricorn!"

"Does the new baby have a brain or has God switched to the Intel Pentium processor?"

"I just joined a support group for Internet addicts. We meet every night from 7:00 until midnight on CompuServe."

"The boss called me an **IDIOT** again today. Just for that, I'm going to erase all his files!"

"Hello, Bob? It's your father again. I have another question about my new computer. Can I tape a movie from cable TV, then fax it from my VCR to my CD-ROM then e-mail it to my brother's cellular phone so he can make a copy on his neighbor's camcorder?"

"Those nudie pictures on the Internet mean nothing to me, Phyllis. You'll always be my HOT BABE OF THE DAY!"

"They gave me these video tapes to help me set up my new computer, but I still haven't figured out how to set up the VCR."

"I made a list of all your good points and all of my computer's good points and I've decided to go steady with my computer."

"Last month we told them to rotate the stock in the warehouse. But the orders they got said 'rotate the warehouse'. Yep, this is gonna cost us."

"I'm tall, dynamic, level-headed and have an electric personality. Looking for a bride. Reply to Frankie@Igor.com"

"How shall I torture you today? Put you on the rack? Boil you in oil? Make you call a technical support line?"

"My new word processor automatically checks my documents for spelling, grammar and political correctness."

"According to my Home Medic CD-ROM, the proper first aid
treatment for a heart attack victim is– Oh darn, I crashed!
Hang on, Sweetie, while I reboot!"

"Howie, I am breaking up with you and moving out.
For more details, please visit my new web site at
http://www.yousuckdropdead.com"

"I really don't need a faster computer.
I need a computer that works as slow as I do!"

CLICK

GLASBERGEN

"I met this really cute girl online. I've never actually seen her, but her typing looks really cute!"

"If you'd like to bark at a cat, press 1.
If you'd like to bark at a squirrel, press 2.
If you'd like to bark at a truck, press 3..."

"They mentioned something interesting on the news and I wanted to learn more about it, but there weren't any hypertext links for me to click on. I'm starting to hate television."

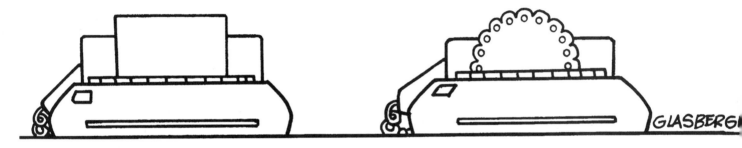

**Plain Paper
Fax Machine.**

**Doily
Fax Machine.**

GLASBERG

"Clifford, I'm afraid we're drifting apart and I think we should discuss it. What's your e-mail address?"

"The boss wants 30% of our stock shipped to Atlanta, 30% to New York, 30% to Chicago and 30% to Los Angeles—and no excuses!"

"I was trying to compress a file and suddenly the whole computer shrank."

The downside of video conferencing.

"Please press 1 to transfer your call. If you're calling from a rotary phone, please make a beepy noise that sounds like you just pressed 1 on a touch-tone phone."

"New regulations: whenever I log into another country, Customs has to inspect my hard drive."

"Daddy is yelling at the computer again.
He needs to install a scream saver."

"Warning: If you keep your web browser at Hot Site Of The Day for too long, your computer may overheat. If this happens, link immediately to Cool Site Of The Day."

"I don't know how old the computers are in my school, but the CD drive uses 8-track tapes."

"I've been on hold since last Thursday.
Do I get paid overtime for this?"

"I asked my dad where babies come from.
He says you download them from the Internet."

"I tapped into the school's computer and changed all my grades. Then the school tapped into my computer and changed all my games to educational programs!"

"No kidding? I'm a sperm cell? Gross!
Up until now, I thought I was a computer mouse!"

"I've got a customer who's turning 40 tomorrow.
He wants to know if we can ship him back to 1965!"

"I was on the Internet this week
and I discovered 24 new sins!"

"Please press 1 to transfer your call. If you are calling
from a rotary phone, hang up and go buy a
new telephone for Pete's sake!"

"The computer made a little mistake today. We were supposed to order the trucks to get loaded at 11:00 AM, but we accidentally order the truckers to get loaded at 11:00 AM."

"I discovered I can speed up my computer by 50%
if I allocate more RAM, close any unnecessary files,
and soak all of my disks in coffee every morning."

"I never made it out of bed this morning.
My body crashed while it was booting up."

"My dad is afraid that hackers will read his private e-mail, so he sends his messages one alphabet letter at a time, in random sequence."

"I found something really gross and disgusting on the Internet–my school lunch menu!"

"Our billing system was perfect until the boss put in his two-cents worth. Now all of our figures are off by two cents."

"He's a great customer, but he's very thrifty.
He wants us to e-mail five tons of freight to Cleveland."

"Maybe that explains why we got it so cheap.
It's a cellulite phone."

"I've identified our productivity problem–
We installed faster computers, but we forgot
to install faster computer operators."

"I thought I could buy stuff over the Internet by sticking my credit card in the floppy disk drive."

"Of course I love my computer more than I love you!
The computer responds when I touch it!"

"There is <u>so</u> such a word as 'XZLOPYF'. While you were in the bathroom, I went on the Internet, logged into Webster's Dictionary and registered 'XZLOPYF' as a brand new word!"

**"YES! Here's what we're looking for–
How To Jump Over The Moon!"**

"At first I felt strange talking to your answering machine.
Once I got used to it, I began to enjoy it.
Now I talk to dishwashers, vacuum cleaners, toasters...
it's so much easier than talking to people!"

"Whenever something goes wrong, I just push this little button and restart. I wish my whole life was like that!"

**"Your order was shipped last week.
However, according to our shipping records,
last week doesn't begin until next Thursday."**

"Whenever I crash, an airbag goes off, so I don't bang my head in frustration."

"My husband passed away eight months ago, but we still keep in touch. His e-mail address is WalterZ@Heaven.com"

"To transfer you call, press #1. To confirm that you have presse #1, press #2. To activate #2, press #3. To confirm that #2 has been properly activated to confirm #1, please press #4..."

"I had to print my new business cards a little bigger to make room for my name, address, phone number, fax number, modem number, Internet address, CompuServe address, America Online address, World Wide Web address..."

"Darling, whenever we're alone together I feel like
I'm being unfaithful to my computer."

"I've gathered the e-mail addresses of every household in North America that owns a cat. Now we can do some serious flaming!"

"As promised, you'll have free use of the company golf course during your lunch hour. Just double-click on the icon labeled 'GOLF'."

GLASBERGEN

"You have reached the Mathematics Department. Professor Kelly is out right now. To leave a message, please press 12875-3901÷4973.99995 x 43/96Y + 45X."

"My History professor told me to use the Internet for research and it's been very helpful. I've located seventeen people who have offered to sell me a term paper!"

"It has 2 megs of RAM, a 15 MB hard drive, it runs at a blazing 10 MHz and best of all, it was on sale this week for just $99!"

"You said to leave a message after the beep.
Was that a beep? It sounded more like a ding.
Is it okay to leave a message after the ding or should
I wait for a real beep? Call me back and let me know."

"That's not my screen saver, that's vomit. I just saw something on the Internet that really grossed me out!"

"And <u>this</u> button gives the computer
a mild electric shock when I need to punish it."

"You have reached the Procrastinator's Support Group. For information about our meetings, please call back another time and press 1 whenever you feel like it."

"If you raise my allowance, I'll show you where all the dirty stuff is on the Internet!"

"You stick your nose into the fax machine, then press START. It works just like the transporter on Star Trek!"

GLASBERGEN

"You spend way too much money on that machine!
The next time you upgrade to a better computer,
I'm upgrading to a better husband!"

"It's amazing what you can find on the Internet. Here's a discussion group for left-handed short people who like to collect autographed ear wax from the pets of celebrity stunt doubles."

"I'm not up on all this new technology.
For the longest time, I thought 'fax you' was an insult."

"I'm doing a Vulcan mind-meld so I can learn everything the computer knows about math before I take my test tomorrow."

**"I taught him how to type W-O-O-F.
Now he can bark at strangers all over the Internet!"**

"I bought him a modem for his computer.
The package said 'for internal use'
...so he swallowed it."

"Technology has made my job much easier! I begin each morning by listening to all my voice mail and when I'm done with that it's time to go home!"

"My parents figured out I was looking at Internet porn.
Every time they turn on the computer, I start drooling."

"Don't forget—you have to install screen Windows for summer and storm Windows for winter."

"I need a Get Well card for my aunt.
She hurt her mouth trying to fax me a kiss."

"I thought the boss was chewing me out,
but then I realized I was sitting on the paper shredder."

"After you've been working hard all day, this program gives your computer a little buzz during Happy Hour."

GLASBERGEN

"Thank you for calling. Please leave a message. In case I forget to check my messages, please send your message as an audio le to my e-mail, then send me a fax to remind me to check my e-mail, then call back to remind me to check my fax."

"Trust me, if we search the Internet long enough we're bound to find dirty pictures of famous movie and TV dogs!"

"My term paper is 15 pages long! Actually it's only 2 pages without the 48 point bold fonts."

"He's been working late a lot with his computer.
I don't know what's going on, but last night he came
home with software on his breath!"

"It's a copier, scanner, fax, printer and voice mail all in one. It's a faster and more efficient way to screw everything up."

"My dad is afraid I'm turning into a computer weenie, so I told him I joined the trackball team."

"To leave a message, press 1. For technical support, press 2.
To send a mild electric shock to our customer
relations manager, press 3."

"Peter, you never <u>talk</u> to me anymore.
All you ever do is point and click!"

"I think pornography on the Internet is a big problem.
My parents won't let me look at it–that's the problem!"

"A guy on TV says we should back up our files.
You think three inches is back far enough?"

"...If you'd like to pass the time by speaking to someone else who's on hold, press 4."

"Roger is witty, charming, handsome, considerate, intelligent, successful, gentle and the most perfect man I ever met. But we had to break up– he's Windows and I'm Mac."

"This is the most powerful computer we sell.
Just be careful not to expose it to kryptonite."

"Let me know right away if the pregnancy test is positive. I want to get started on the baby's web page."

"My brother just got a big raise and a promotion. To celebrate, he put up a new web page at http://www.kissmyass.com"

As 3-D graphics become more sophisticated, web pages will continue to evolve and affect the way we interact with others.

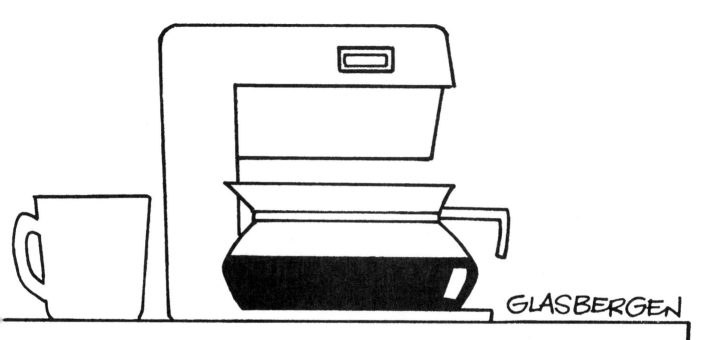

Because of his ongoing ability to increase office productivity, the "Employee Of The Month" award again goes to Mr. Coffee.